50 Nourishing Bowl Recipes

By: Kelly Johnson

Table of Contents

- Quinoa and Black Bean Bowl
- Brown Rice Buddha Bowl
- Lentil and Sweet Potato Bowl
- Mediterranean Chickpea Bowl
- Thai Peanut Noodle Bowl
- Teriyaki Salmon Bowl
- Tofu and Vegetable Stir-Fry Bowl
- Chicken and Avocado Rice Bowl
- Moroccan Spiced Grain Bowl
- Spinach and Feta Quinoa Bowl
- Curried Cauliflower and Chickpeas Bowl
- Shrimp and Asparagus Bowl
- BBQ Chicken and Corn Bowl
- Pesto Zoodle Bowl
- Greek Yogurt Breakfast Bowl
- Salmon Poke Bowl
- Beef and Broccoli Rice Bowl
- Falafel and Tahini Bowl
- Roasted Vegetable and Hummus Bowl
- Caprese Quinoa Bowl
- Smoked Salmon and Avocado Bowl
- Sautéed Kale and Sweet Potato Bowl
- Mexican Street Corn Bowl
- Coconut Curry Chickpea Bowl
- Kimchi Fried Rice Bowl
- Chicken Caesar Salad Bowl
- Wild Rice and Cranberry Bowl
- Ratatouille Grain Bowl
- Balsamic Chicken and Veggie Bowl
- Egg and Spinach Breakfast Bowl
- Miso Ramen Bowl
- Szechuan Noodles and Veggies Bowl
- Zucchini Noodle Bowl
- Thai Coconut Curry Rice Bowl
- Grilled Vegetable Quinoa Bowl
- Cabbage and Chicken Bowl

- Tuna Poke Bowl
- Creamy Avocado and Tomato Bowl
- Sweet Potato and Kale Bowl
- Cilantro Lime Rice Bowl
- Mushroom and Barley Bowl
- Lemon Herb Chicken Bowl
- Roasted Beet and Goat Cheese Bowl
- Breakfast Chia Seed Bowl
- Quinoa and Roasted Red Pepper Bowl
- Spicy Lentil and Rice Bowl
- Chickpea Salad Bowl
- Tomato Basil Pasta Bowl
- Teriyaki Tofu and Broccoli Bowl
- Harvest Grain and Apple Bowl

Quinoa and Black Bean Bowl

Ingredients

- 1 cup quinoa, rinsed
- 2 cups vegetable broth
- 1 can black beans, drained and rinsed
- 1 cup corn kernels
- 1 bell pepper, diced
- 1 avocado, sliced
- 1 lime, juiced
- Salt and pepper to taste
- Fresh cilantro for garnish

Instructions

1. **Cook Quinoa:** In a pot, bring vegetable broth to a boil. Add quinoa, reduce heat, cover, and simmer for 15 minutes or until liquid is absorbed.
2. **Combine Ingredients:** In a bowl, combine cooked quinoa, black beans, corn, and diced bell pepper.
3. **Season:** Drizzle with lime juice, and season with salt and pepper.
4. **Serve:** Top with avocado slices and garnish with fresh cilantro.

Brown Rice Buddha Bowl

Ingredients

- 1 cup brown rice, cooked
- 1 cup roasted vegetables (carrots, zucchini, bell peppers)
- 1/2 cup chickpeas, drained and rinsed
- 1/4 avocado, sliced
- 2 tbsp tahini dressing
- Fresh spinach or kale
- Salt and pepper to taste

Instructions

1. **Prepare Base:** In a bowl, place a base of cooked brown rice.
2. **Add Vegetables:** Layer roasted vegetables and chickpeas on top.
3. **Top It Off:** Add avocado slices and a handful of fresh spinach or kale.
4. **Drizzle Dressing:** Drizzle with tahini dressing and season with salt and pepper.

Lentil and Sweet Potato Bowl

Ingredients

- 1 cup lentils, rinsed
- 1 medium sweet potato, cubed
- 1 tsp olive oil
- 1/2 tsp cumin
- 1/2 tsp paprika
- Salt and pepper to taste
- Fresh parsley for garnish

Instructions

1. **Cook Lentils:** In a pot, cover lentils with water and bring to a boil. Reduce heat and simmer for 20-25 minutes until tender.
2. **Roast Sweet Potatoes:** Toss cubed sweet potatoes in olive oil, cumin, paprika, salt, and pepper. Roast at 400°F (200°C) for 25-30 minutes.
3. **Combine and Serve:** In a bowl, combine lentils and roasted sweet potatoes. Garnish with fresh parsley.

Mediterranean Chickpea Bowl

Ingredients

- 1 can chickpeas, drained and rinsed
- 1 cup cherry tomatoes, halved
- 1 cucumber, diced
- 1/4 red onion, finely chopped
- 1/4 cup feta cheese, crumbled
- 2 tbsp olive oil
- 1 tbsp lemon juice
- Salt and pepper to taste
- Fresh parsley for garnish

Instructions

1. **Combine Ingredients:** In a bowl, mix chickpeas, cherry tomatoes, cucumber, red onion, and feta cheese.
2. **Dress the Bowl:** Drizzle with olive oil and lemon juice, and season with salt and pepper.
3. **Garnish:** Toss gently and garnish with fresh parsley.

Thai Peanut Noodle Bowl

Ingredients

- 8 oz rice noodles
- 1 cup mixed vegetables (bell peppers, carrots, snap peas)
- 1/2 cup peanut sauce
- 2 green onions, sliced
- 1/4 cup crushed peanuts
- Lime wedges for serving

Instructions

1. **Cook Noodles:** Prepare rice noodles according to package instructions.
2. **Sauté Vegetables:** In a pan, sauté mixed vegetables until tender.
3. **Combine:** Add cooked noodles and peanut sauce to the pan, tossing to coat.
4. **Serve:** Divide into bowls, topping with green onions and crushed peanuts, and serve with lime wedges.

Teriyaki Salmon Bowl

Ingredients

- 2 salmon fillets
- 1/4 cup teriyaki sauce
- 2 cups steamed broccoli
- 1 cup cooked rice (white or brown)
- Sesame seeds for garnish

Instructions

1. **Marinate Salmon:** Marinate salmon fillets in teriyaki sauce for at least 15 minutes.
2. **Cook Salmon:** Grill or pan-sear salmon until cooked through, about 4-5 minutes per side.
3. **Assemble Bowl:** In a bowl, layer rice, steamed broccoli, and salmon.
4. **Garnish:** Drizzle with additional teriyaki sauce and sprinkle with sesame seeds.

Tofu and Vegetable Stir-Fry Bowl

Ingredients

- 1 block firm tofu, cubed
- 2 cups mixed vegetables (bell peppers, broccoli, carrots)
- 2 tbsp soy sauce
- 1 tbsp sesame oil
- Cooked rice or quinoa for serving

Instructions

1. **Sauté Tofu:** In a pan, heat sesame oil and add cubed tofu. Cook until golden brown.
2. **Add Vegetables:** Stir in mixed vegetables and cook until tender.
3. **Season:** Add soy sauce and toss to combine.
4. **Serve:** Serve over cooked rice or quinoa.

Chicken and Avocado Rice Bowl

Ingredients

- 2 chicken breasts, grilled and sliced
- 1 cup cooked rice
- 1 avocado, sliced
- 1/2 cup cherry tomatoes, halved
- 1/4 cup cilantro, chopped
- Lime wedges for serving

Instructions

1. **Prepare Base:** In a bowl, place a base of cooked rice.
2. **Add Chicken and Veggies:** Top with sliced chicken, avocado, and cherry tomatoes.
3. **Garnish:** Sprinkle with chopped cilantro and serve with lime wedges.

Moroccan Spiced Grain Bowl

Ingredients

- 1 cup cooked quinoa or couscous
- 1 cup roasted vegetables (zucchini, carrots, bell peppers)
- 1 can chickpeas, drained and rinsed
- 1 tsp Moroccan spice blend (cumin, coriander, cinnamon)
- 1/4 cup dried apricots, chopped
- 1/4 cup slivered almonds
- Fresh cilantro for garnish
- Olive oil, for drizzling

Instructions

1. **Prepare Base:** In a bowl, place the cooked quinoa or couscous.
2. **Mix Ingredients:** Top with roasted vegetables and chickpeas.
3. **Season:** Sprinkle with Moroccan spice blend, dried apricots, and slivered almonds.
4. **Finish:** Drizzle with olive oil and garnish with fresh cilantro.

Spinach and Feta Quinoa Bowl

Ingredients

- 1 cup cooked quinoa
- 2 cups fresh spinach
- 1/2 cup feta cheese, crumbled
- 1/2 cup cherry tomatoes, halved
- 1/4 cup olives, sliced
- 2 tbsp olive oil
- 1 tbsp lemon juice
- Salt and pepper to taste

Instructions

1. **Combine Ingredients:** In a bowl, mix cooked quinoa, fresh spinach, feta cheese, cherry tomatoes, and olives.
2. **Dress the Bowl:** Drizzle with olive oil and lemon juice.
3. **Season:** Season with salt and pepper to taste and toss gently.

Curried Cauliflower and Chickpeas Bowl

Ingredients

- 1 head cauliflower, cut into florets
- 1 can chickpeas, drained and rinsed
- 2 tbsp curry powder
- 1 tbsp olive oil
- 1 cup cooked brown rice
- Fresh cilantro for garnish

Instructions

1. **Roast Vegetables:** Preheat oven to 400°F (200°C). Toss cauliflower and chickpeas with olive oil and curry powder. Spread on a baking sheet and roast for 20-25 minutes.
2. **Prepare Base:** In a bowl, place a base of cooked brown rice.
3. **Add Roasted Veggies:** Top with roasted cauliflower and chickpeas.
4. **Garnish:** Sprinkle with fresh cilantro before serving.

Shrimp and Asparagus Bowl

Ingredients

- 1 lb shrimp, peeled and deveined
- 1 bunch asparagus, trimmed and cut into pieces
- 2 cloves garlic, minced
- 1 tbsp olive oil
- 1 cup cooked rice or quinoa
- Lemon wedges for serving
- Salt and pepper to taste

Instructions

1. **Sauté Shrimp:** In a skillet, heat olive oil over medium heat. Add garlic and shrimp, cooking until shrimp are pink and opaque.
2. **Add Asparagus:** Add asparagus and cook for an additional 3-4 minutes until tender.
3. **Prepare Bowl:** In a bowl, place cooked rice or quinoa and top with shrimp and asparagus.
4. **Finish:** Season with salt and pepper and serve with lemon wedges.

BBQ Chicken and Corn Bowl

Ingredients

- 2 cups cooked shredded chicken
- 1 cup corn kernels (fresh or canned)
- 1/2 cup BBQ sauce
- 1 cup cooked brown rice
- 1/4 cup green onions, sliced
- 1/4 cup cilantro for garnish

Instructions

1. **Mix Chicken:** In a bowl, combine shredded chicken with BBQ sauce and corn.
2. **Prepare Base:** In a separate bowl, place cooked brown rice as the base.
3. **Top It Off:** Add the BBQ chicken mixture on top of the rice.
4. **Garnish:** Sprinkle with green onions and fresh cilantro.

Pesto Zoodle Bowl

Ingredients

- 4 medium zucchini, spiralized into noodles
- 1 cup cherry tomatoes, halved
- 1/4 cup pesto sauce
- 1/4 cup pine nuts, toasted
- Grated Parmesan cheese for serving

Instructions

1. **Sauté Zoodles:** In a skillet, lightly sauté zucchini noodles over medium heat for 2-3 minutes until just tender.
2. **Combine Ingredients:** In a bowl, mix zoodles with cherry tomatoes and pesto sauce.
3. **Top It Off:** Sprinkle with toasted pine nuts and grated Parmesan cheese before serving.

Greek Yogurt Breakfast Bowl

Ingredients

- 1 cup Greek yogurt
- 1/2 cup granola
- 1/2 cup mixed berries (strawberries, blueberries, raspberries)
- 1 tbsp honey
- Mint leaves for garnish

Instructions

1. **Prepare Base:** In a bowl, place Greek yogurt as the base.
2. **Add Toppings:** Top with granola and mixed berries.
3. **Drizzle:** Drizzle with honey and garnish with mint leaves before serving.

Salmon Poke Bowl

Ingredients

- 1 lb sushi-grade salmon, diced
- 1 cup cooked rice (white or brown)
- 1 avocado, sliced
- 1/2 cucumber, thinly sliced
- 2 green onions, sliced
- 2 tbsp soy sauce
- Sesame seeds for garnish

Instructions

1. **Prepare Base:** In a bowl, place a base of cooked rice.
2. **Add Toppings:** Top with diced salmon, avocado slices, cucumber, and green onions.
3. **Season:** Drizzle with soy sauce and garnish with sesame seeds before serving.

Beef and Broccoli Rice Bowl

Ingredients

- 1 lb beef sirloin, thinly sliced
- 2 cups broccoli florets
- 2 cups cooked rice
- 3 tbsp soy sauce
- 1 tbsp oyster sauce
- 1 tsp cornstarch mixed with 1 tbsp water
- 2 cloves garlic, minced
- 1 tbsp vegetable oil
- Sesame seeds for garnish

Instructions

1. **Stir-Fry Beef:** In a skillet, heat vegetable oil over medium-high heat. Add garlic and stir-fry until fragrant, then add beef and cook until browned.
2. **Add Broccoli:** Stir in broccoli and cook for an additional 3-4 minutes until tender.
3. **Mix Sauces:** Add soy sauce, oyster sauce, and the cornstarch mixture. Stir well until the sauce thickens.
4. **Serve:** Place cooked rice in a bowl and top with the beef and broccoli mixture. Garnish with sesame seeds.

Falafel and Tahini Bowl

Ingredients

- 1 cup cooked chickpeas
- 1/4 cup fresh parsley, chopped
- 1/4 cup onion, diced
- 2 cloves garlic, minced
- 1 tsp cumin
- 1/2 tsp coriander
- 1/4 cup flour
- Olive oil for frying
- 1/2 cup tahini sauce
- Mixed greens for serving

Instructions

1. **Prepare Falafel Mixture:** In a food processor, blend chickpeas, parsley, onion, garlic, cumin, coriander, and flour until combined.
2. **Form Falafel:** Shape the mixture into small balls or patties.
3. **Fry Falafel:** In a skillet, heat olive oil over medium heat. Fry falafel until golden brown on all sides.
4. **Assemble Bowl:** Serve falafel on a bed of mixed greens and drizzle with tahini sauce.

Roasted Vegetable and Hummus Bowl

Ingredients

- 2 cups mixed vegetables (bell peppers, zucchini, carrots), chopped
- 2 tbsp olive oil
- Salt and pepper to taste
- 1 cup cooked quinoa
- 1/2 cup hummus
- Fresh parsley for garnish

Instructions

1. **Roast Vegetables:** Preheat oven to 400°F (200°C). Toss vegetables with olive oil, salt, and pepper, and spread on a baking sheet. Roast for 20-25 minutes.
2. **Prepare Base:** In a bowl, place cooked quinoa as the base.
3. **Add Roasted Veggies:** Top quinoa with roasted vegetables and a generous scoop of hummus.
4. **Garnish:** Sprinkle with fresh parsley before serving.

Caprese Quinoa Bowl

Ingredients

- 1 cup cooked quinoa
- 1 cup cherry tomatoes, halved
- 1 cup mozzarella balls
- Fresh basil leaves
- 2 tbsp balsamic glaze
- Olive oil, for drizzling
- Salt and pepper to taste

Instructions

1. **Combine Ingredients:** In a bowl, mix cooked quinoa, cherry tomatoes, mozzarella balls, and fresh basil.
2. **Dress the Bowl:** Drizzle with balsamic glaze and olive oil.
3. **Season:** Add salt and pepper to taste, and toss gently before serving.

Smoked Salmon and Avocado Bowl

Ingredients

- 1 cup cooked brown rice
- 4 oz smoked salmon
- 1 avocado, sliced
- 1/2 cucumber, sliced
- 1/4 cup red onion, thinly sliced
- 2 tbsp capers
- Fresh dill for garnish
- Lemon wedges for serving

Instructions

1. **Prepare Base:** In a bowl, place a base of cooked brown rice.
2. **Add Toppings:** Top with smoked salmon, avocado slices, cucumber, red onion, and capers.
3. **Garnish:** Sprinkle with fresh dill and serve with lemon wedges.

Sautéed Kale and Sweet Potato Bowl

Ingredients

- 1 medium sweet potato, diced
- 2 cups kale, chopped
- 1 tbsp olive oil
- 1/2 tsp smoked paprika
- Salt and pepper to taste
- 1 cup cooked quinoa

Instructions

1. **Roast Sweet Potato:** Preheat oven to 425°F (220°C). Toss sweet potato with olive oil, smoked paprika, salt, and pepper. Roast for 25-30 minutes until tender.
2. **Sauté Kale:** In a skillet, add a bit more olive oil and sauté kale until wilted.
3. **Assemble Bowl:** In a bowl, layer cooked quinoa, roasted sweet potato, and sautéed kale. Serve warm.

Mexican Street Corn Bowl

Ingredients

- 2 cups corn kernels (fresh or canned)
- 1/4 cup mayonnaise
- 1/4 cup crumbled cotija cheese
- 1 lime, juiced
- 1/4 tsp chili powder
- Fresh cilantro for garnish
- 1 cup cooked rice

Instructions

1. **Mix Corn Salad:** In a bowl, combine corn, mayonnaise, cotija cheese, lime juice, and chili powder.
2. **Prepare Base:** In a separate bowl, place cooked rice as the base.
3. **Top It Off:** Add the corn mixture on top of the rice and garnish with fresh cilantro.

Coconut Curry Chickpea Bowl

Ingredients

- 1 can chickpeas, drained and rinsed
- 1 can coconut milk
- 2 tbsp curry powder
- 1 cup spinach
- 1 cup cooked quinoa
- Fresh cilantro for garnish

Instructions

1. **Cook Chickpeas:** In a saucepan, combine chickpeas, coconut milk, and curry powder. Simmer for 10-15 minutes.
2. **Add Spinach:** Stir in spinach until wilted.
3. **Prepare Bowl:** In a bowl, place cooked quinoa and top with the coconut curry chickpeas.
4. **Garnish:** Sprinkle with fresh cilantro before serving.

Kimchi Fried Rice Bowl

Ingredients

- 2 cups cooked rice
- 1 cup kimchi, chopped
- 2 eggs, lightly beaten
- 1/2 cup green onions, sliced
- 2 tbsp soy sauce
- 1 tbsp sesame oil
- Sesame seeds for garnish

Instructions

1. **Sauté Kimchi:** In a skillet, heat sesame oil over medium heat. Add chopped kimchi and stir-fry for about 2-3 minutes.
2. **Add Rice:** Stir in the cooked rice and soy sauce, mixing well to combine. Cook for another 3-4 minutes until heated through.
3. **Cook Eggs:** Push rice to one side of the pan, pour in beaten eggs, and scramble until cooked. Mix with the rice.
4. **Serve:** Top with sliced green onions and sesame seeds before serving.

Chicken Caesar Salad Bowl

Ingredients

- 2 cups romaine lettuce, chopped
- 1 cup cooked chicken breast, sliced
- 1/2 cup Caesar dressing
- 1/4 cup Parmesan cheese, grated
- Croutons for topping

Instructions

1. **Combine Salad:** In a large bowl, combine chopped romaine lettuce, sliced chicken, and Caesar dressing. Toss to coat evenly.
2. **Add Cheese:** Sprinkle with grated Parmesan cheese and toss again.
3. **Serve:** Top with croutons before serving.

Wild Rice and Cranberry Bowl

Ingredients

- 1 cup cooked wild rice
- 1/2 cup dried cranberries
- 1/4 cup walnuts, chopped
- 1/4 cup green onions, sliced
- 2 tbsp olive oil
- Salt and pepper to taste

Instructions

1. **Mix Ingredients:** In a bowl, combine cooked wild rice, dried cranberries, chopped walnuts, and sliced green onions.
2. **Dress the Bowl:** Drizzle with olive oil and season with salt and pepper. Toss gently to mix.
3. **Serve:** Enjoy as a hearty and healthy bowl.

Ratatouille Grain Bowl

Ingredients

- 1 cup cooked quinoa or brown rice
- 1 zucchini, diced
- 1 bell pepper, diced
- 1 eggplant, diced
- 1 can diced tomatoes
- 2 cloves garlic, minced
- 1 tsp dried herbs (thyme, basil, or oregano)
- Olive oil for cooking

Instructions

1. **Sauté Vegetables:** In a skillet, heat olive oil over medium heat. Add garlic and sauté until fragrant. Add zucchini, bell pepper, and eggplant, cooking until tender.
2. **Add Tomatoes:** Stir in diced tomatoes and herbs, cooking for an additional 5-7 minutes.
3. **Assemble Bowl:** In a bowl, place cooked quinoa or brown rice as the base and top with the ratatouille mixture.

Balsamic Chicken and Veggie Bowl

Ingredients

- 1 cup cooked chicken, diced
- 1 cup mixed vegetables (bell peppers, broccoli, carrots)
- 3 tbsp balsamic vinegar
- 1 tbsp olive oil
- Salt and pepper to taste
- Cooked brown rice for serving

Instructions

1. **Sauté Vegetables:** In a skillet, heat olive oil over medium heat. Add mixed vegetables and cook until tender.
2. **Add Chicken:** Stir in diced chicken and balsamic vinegar, cooking until heated through. Season with salt and pepper.
3. **Serve:** Place cooked brown rice in a bowl and top with the chicken and vegetable mixture.

Egg and Spinach Breakfast Bowl

Ingredients

- 2 eggs
- 2 cups fresh spinach
- 1/2 avocado, sliced
- 1/4 cup cherry tomatoes, halved
- Salt and pepper to taste
- Cooked quinoa or toast for serving

Instructions

1. **Cook Eggs:** In a skillet, cook eggs to your liking (poached, scrambled, or fried).
2. **Sauté Spinach:** In the same skillet, sauté spinach until wilted.
3. **Assemble Bowl:** In a bowl, layer cooked quinoa or toast, topped with sautéed spinach, eggs, avocado slices, and cherry tomatoes. Season with salt and pepper.

Miso Ramen Bowl

Ingredients

- 4 cups vegetable or chicken broth
- 2 tbsp miso paste
- 2 servings ramen noodles
- 1 cup sliced mushrooms
- 2 green onions, sliced
- Soft-boiled eggs for topping
- Seaweed for garnish

Instructions

1. **Prepare Broth:** In a pot, bring broth to a simmer and whisk in miso paste until dissolved.
2. **Cook Noodles:** Add ramen noodles and sliced mushrooms to the broth, cooking until noodles are tender.
3. **Serve:** Ladle into bowls and top with green onions, soft-boiled eggs, and seaweed.

Szechuan Noodles and Veggies Bowl

Ingredients

- 8 oz noodles (your choice)
- 2 cups mixed vegetables (carrots, bell peppers, snap peas)
- 3 tbsp Szechuan sauce
- 1 tbsp sesame oil
- 2 cloves garlic, minced
- Chopped peanuts for garnish

Instructions

1. **Cook Noodles:** Prepare noodles according to package instructions, then drain.
2. **Sauté Veggies:** In a skillet, heat sesame oil and sauté garlic and mixed vegetables until tender.
3. **Combine:** Add noodles and Szechuan sauce to the skillet, tossing to combine.
4. **Serve:** Transfer to a bowl and top with chopped peanuts before serving.

Zucchini Noodle Bowl

Ingredients

- 2 medium zucchinis, spiralized
- 1 cup cherry tomatoes, halved
- 1/4 cup basil pesto
- 1/4 cup grated Parmesan cheese
- Salt and pepper to taste

Instructions

1. **Sauté Zucchini:** In a skillet over medium heat, sauté the spiralized zucchini noodles for about 2-3 minutes until just tender.
2. **Add Tomatoes:** Stir in cherry tomatoes and cook for another minute.
3. **Combine Ingredients:** Remove from heat, add basil pesto, and toss to coat.
4. **Serve:** Transfer to a bowl, season with salt and pepper, and top with grated Parmesan cheese.

Thai Coconut Curry Rice Bowl

Ingredients

- 1 cup jasmine rice, cooked
- 1 can coconut milk
- 2 tbsp red curry paste
- 1 cup mixed vegetables (bell peppers, broccoli, snap peas)
- Fresh cilantro for garnish

Instructions

1. **Prepare Curry:** In a saucepan, combine coconut milk and red curry paste over medium heat. Stir until smooth.
2. **Add Vegetables:** Add mixed vegetables and simmer for about 5-7 minutes until tender.
3. **Assemble Bowl:** Place cooked jasmine rice in a bowl and top with the coconut curry mixture.
4. **Garnish:** Sprinkle with fresh cilantro before serving.

Grilled Vegetable Quinoa Bowl

Ingredients

- 1 cup cooked quinoa
- 1 zucchini, sliced
- 1 bell pepper, sliced
- 1 cup cherry tomatoes
- 2 tbsp olive oil
- Salt and pepper to taste

Instructions

1. **Grill Vegetables:** Preheat grill. Toss sliced zucchini, bell pepper, and cherry tomatoes with olive oil, salt, and pepper. Grill until tender and slightly charred.
2. **Combine Ingredients:** In a bowl, combine cooked quinoa and grilled vegetables.
3. **Serve:** Mix gently and enjoy warm.

Cabbage and Chicken Bowl

Ingredients

- 2 cups shredded cabbage
- 1 cup cooked chicken, shredded
- 1/4 cup sesame dressing
- 1/4 cup sliced almonds
- Green onions for garnish

Instructions

1. **Mix Bowl:** In a large bowl, combine shredded cabbage, cooked chicken, and sesame dressing. Toss until well combined.
2. **Add Toppings:** Top with sliced almonds and garnish with green onions.
3. **Serve:** Enjoy as a refreshing and hearty bowl.

Tuna Poke Bowl

Ingredients

- 1 cup sushi rice, cooked
- 1 cup fresh tuna, diced
- 1 avocado, sliced
- 1/4 cup soy sauce
- 1 tbsp sesame oil
- Seaweed salad for topping

Instructions

1. **Prepare Tuna:** In a bowl, combine diced tuna, soy sauce, and sesame oil. Let marinate for about 10 minutes.
2. **Assemble Bowl:** Place cooked sushi rice in a bowl and top with marinated tuna, avocado slices, and seaweed salad.
3. **Serve:** Enjoy fresh as a light and delicious meal.

Creamy Avocado and Tomato Bowl

Ingredients

- 2 ripe avocados, mashed
- 1 cup cherry tomatoes, halved
- 1 lime, juiced
- Salt and pepper to taste
- Tortilla chips for serving

Instructions

1. **Mix Ingredients:** In a bowl, combine mashed avocados, halved cherry tomatoes, lime juice, salt, and pepper.
2. **Serve:** Enjoy with tortilla chips for dipping.

Sweet Potato and Kale Bowl

Ingredients

- 1 large sweet potato, cubed
- 2 cups kale, chopped
- 1 tbsp olive oil
- 1/2 tsp smoked paprika
- Salt and pepper to taste

Instructions

1. **Roast Sweet Potatoes:** Preheat oven to 400°F (200°C). Toss cubed sweet potatoes with olive oil, smoked paprika, salt, and pepper. Roast for 25-30 minutes until tender.
2. **Sauté Kale:** In a skillet, sauté chopped kale until wilted.
3. **Assemble Bowl:** In a bowl, layer roasted sweet potatoes and sautéed kale.
4. **Serve:** Enjoy warm as a nutritious meal.

Cilantro Lime Rice Bowl

Ingredients

- 1 cup cooked rice
- 1/4 cup fresh cilantro, chopped
- Juice of 1 lime
- 1/4 cup black beans, drained and rinsed
- Diced tomatoes for topping

Instructions

1. **Mix Rice:** In a bowl, combine cooked rice, chopped cilantro, lime juice, and black beans.
2. **Serve:** Top with diced tomatoes and enjoy as a zesty bowl.

Mushroom and Barley Bowl

Ingredients

- 1 cup pearl barley, cooked
- 2 cups mushrooms, sliced
- 1 cup vegetable broth
- 2 cloves garlic, minced
- 1 tbsp olive oil
- Fresh parsley for garnish

Instructions

1. **Sauté Mushrooms:** In a skillet, heat olive oil over medium heat. Add minced garlic and sliced mushrooms, sautéing until mushrooms are golden brown.
2. **Add Broth:** Pour in vegetable broth and let simmer for 5-7 minutes until slightly thickened.
3. **Combine Ingredients:** In a bowl, combine cooked barley with the mushroom mixture.
4. **Garnish and Serve:** Top with fresh parsley and enjoy warm.

Lemon Herb Chicken Bowl

Ingredients

- 2 cups cooked quinoa
- 1 cup grilled chicken, sliced
- 1/4 cup lemon juice
- 1 tbsp olive oil
- 1 cup mixed greens
- Salt and pepper to taste

Instructions

1. **Prepare Dressing:** In a small bowl, whisk together lemon juice, olive oil, salt, and pepper.
2. **Assemble Bowl:** In a large bowl, combine cooked quinoa, sliced grilled chicken, and mixed greens.
3. **Dress and Serve:** Drizzle with lemon dressing and toss gently before serving.

Roasted Beet and Goat Cheese Bowl

Ingredients

- 2 cups mixed greens
- 1 cup roasted beets, sliced
- 1/4 cup goat cheese, crumbled
- 1/4 cup walnuts, toasted
- Balsamic vinaigrette for dressing

Instructions

1. **Prepare Salad Base:** In a bowl, layer mixed greens, sliced roasted beets, crumbled goat cheese, and toasted walnuts.
2. **Dress and Serve:** Drizzle with balsamic vinaigrette and toss gently before serving.

Breakfast Chia Seed Bowl

Ingredients

- 1/4 cup chia seeds
- 1 cup almond milk (or milk of choice)
- 1 tbsp honey or maple syrup
- Fresh fruit for topping (e.g., berries, banana, kiwi)
- Nuts or granola for crunch

Instructions

1. **Combine Ingredients:** In a bowl, mix chia seeds, almond milk, and honey or maple syrup. Stir well and let sit for at least 30 minutes or overnight in the refrigerator.
2. **Serve:** Top with fresh fruit and nuts or granola before enjoying.

Quinoa and Roasted Red Pepper Bowl

Ingredients

- 1 cup cooked quinoa
- 1 cup roasted red peppers, sliced
- 1/2 cup chickpeas, rinsed and drained
- 1 tbsp olive oil
- 1 tsp paprika
- Fresh basil for garnish

Instructions

1. **Combine Ingredients:** In a bowl, mix cooked quinoa, roasted red peppers, chickpeas, olive oil, and paprika.
2. **Garnish and Serve:** Top with fresh basil and enjoy warm or cold.

Spicy Lentil and Rice Bowl

Ingredients

- 1 cup cooked brown rice
- 1 cup cooked lentils
- 1 tbsp chili powder
- 1/2 tsp cumin
- 1 cup diced tomatoes
- Fresh cilantro for garnish

Instructions

1. **Mix Ingredients:** In a bowl, combine cooked brown rice, cooked lentils, chili powder, cumin, and diced tomatoes.
2. **Garnish and Serve:** Top with fresh cilantro and enjoy warm.

Chickpea Salad Bowl

Ingredients

- 1 can chickpeas, drained and rinsed
- 1 cup diced cucumber
- 1 cup cherry tomatoes, halved
- 1/4 cup red onion, finely chopped
- Juice of 1 lemon
- Olive oil, salt, and pepper to taste

Instructions

1. **Mix Salad:** In a large bowl, combine chickpeas, cucumber, cherry tomatoes, and red onion.
2. **Dress and Serve:** Drizzle with lemon juice, olive oil, salt, and pepper. Toss gently and enjoy.

Tomato Basil Pasta Bowl

Ingredients

- 2 cups cooked pasta (your choice)
- 1 cup cherry tomatoes, halved
- 1/4 cup fresh basil, chopped
- 1 tbsp olive oil
- Salt and pepper to taste
- Grated Parmesan for topping

Instructions

1. **Combine Ingredients:** In a bowl, mix cooked pasta, cherry tomatoes, fresh basil, olive oil, salt, and pepper.
2. **Serve:** Top with grated Parmesan cheese and enjoy warm.

Teriyaki Tofu and Broccoli Bowl

Ingredients

- 1 block firm tofu, pressed and cubed
- 2 cups broccoli florets
- 1/4 cup teriyaki sauce
- 1 tbsp olive oil
- 1 cup cooked rice (white or brown)
- Sesame seeds for garnish
- Green onions, sliced for garnish

Instructions

1. **Sauté Tofu:** In a skillet, heat olive oil over medium heat. Add cubed tofu and sauté until golden brown on all sides.
2. **Add Broccoli:** Add broccoli florets to the skillet and cook for 3-4 minutes until tender.
3. **Stir in Sauce:** Pour teriyaki sauce over the tofu and broccoli, stirring to coat everything evenly. Cook for an additional 2-3 minutes.
4. **Assemble Bowl:** Serve the tofu and broccoli over cooked rice, garnished with sesame seeds and sliced green onions.

Harvest Grain and Apple Bowl

Ingredients

- 1 cup cooked farro or quinoa
- 1 apple, diced (any variety)
- 1/2 cup dried cranberries
- 1/4 cup pecans, chopped
- 1/4 cup feta cheese, crumbled (optional)
- 2 tbsp olive oil
- 1 tbsp apple cider vinegar
- Salt and pepper to taste

Instructions

1. **Combine Ingredients:** In a large bowl, mix cooked farro or quinoa, diced apple, dried cranberries, chopped pecans, and feta cheese (if using).
2. **Dress and Serve:** Drizzle with olive oil and apple cider vinegar, and season with salt and pepper. Toss gently and enjoy as a warm or cold dish.

www.ingramcontent.com/pod-product-compliance
Lightning Source LLC
LaVergne TN
LVHW081342060526
838201LV00055B/2804